SKETCHES OF ST

Sue Lewington

The Church & the new Lifeboat House.

Sue Lewington is a working artist & has lived in Cornwall for many years. She has her own Gallery on St. Martins, Isles of Scilly & her paintings are to be found in many collections.

For Sue it is essential that she work out of doors so that she can "catch the moment" - whether it be a broad vista or the small domestic detail.

Published by Dyllansow Truran, Croft Prince, Mount Hawke, Truro, Cornwall TR4 8EE

Printed by R. Booth at the Troutbeck Press, Antron Hill, Mabe, Penryn, Cornwall, TR10 9HH

ISBN   1   85022   118 9 (paperback)
ISBN   1   85022   119 7 (cased)

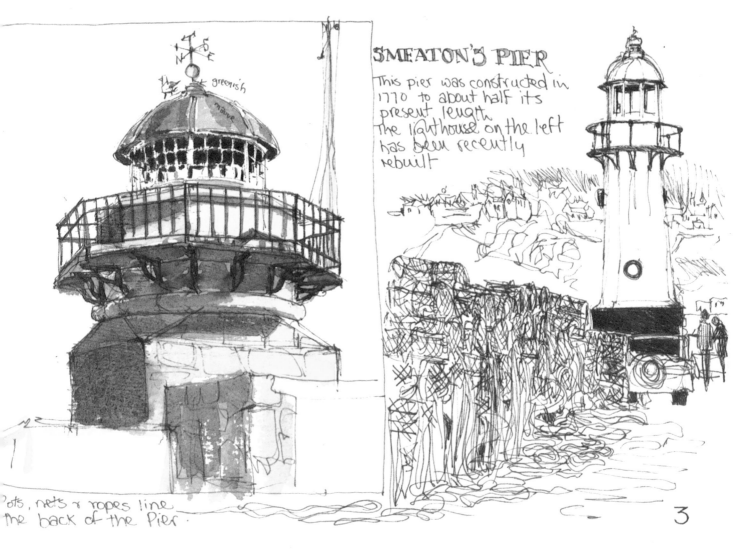

greenish

above

SMEATON'S PIER

This pier was constructed in
1770 to about half its
present length
The lighthouse on the left
has been recently
rebuilt

Pots, nets & ropes line
the back of the pier.

Men at work. Theres no rush, no panic - they all seem relaxed, just quietly getting on

4

5

6   More backstreets .   Railings   and washing

on a cottage in Virgin St.

COTTAGE
STREET IVES

I hope this one is true
↓

ATMOSPHERE
DOMINATES
THE ATTITUDE

sometimes its the other way round!

and on a Gallery door.

7

8

A lazy morning - early...
mist lifting, sun getting warmer.

The SHELL SHOP

baskets of starfish
along the pavement

10

Fruit cakes & heavy cakes, apple pies &
saffron buns..

...re are tiny shops everywhere

FLOWERS

...AL SHOP

FRESH FRUIT AND VEGETABLES

...FORE STORE

fruit & veg. Homemade pies, jams, cheese - everything in a tiny shop

Alfred Wallis' house, with a
plaque by the door

ALFRED WALLIS
ARTIST & MARINER
1855 - 1942
LIVED HERE

Just round the corner from Porthmeor Beach & the Tate

ALFRED WALLIS
ARTIST & MARINER
1855   aug 18 aug 29   1942
INTO THY HANDS O LORD...

Everything in St. Ives is built on a hill
even Alfred Wallis' grave...
Overlooking Porthmeor   with the sound
of the waves & the gulls for
company...

It didn't look like this when he lived here....

12

All the gulls suddenly take to the air, screaming & crying - answered by the gulls on the roof.

SAINT LEONARD'S CHAPEL
The Traditional Chapel of the Fishermen of St Ives

ST. LEONARD'S CHAPEL
The traditional chapel of the fishermen of St. Ives.

PLEASE DO NOT TAP THE WINDOW

A notice pinned to the barometer case INSIDE the window

The notice-board is full of faded pieces of paper advertising boats for sale

13

LOVE LANE

GALLERY

Backstreets

14

St. Ives is full of wonderful street names
— The Digey, Teetotal street, Virgin street,
Bethesda Place, Salubrious Terrace, Court Cocking, Fish street, Pudding Bag Lane, Rose Lane

I keep finding corners I havent seen before.

15

TENDER FOR TRINKET

our Daddy St Ives

weathervane on the Lifeboat House

SS 272

The church & the new Lifeboat House.

16

utside the Lifeboat House.

The new   & Old Lifeboat Houses

17

THE BARBARA HEPWORTH MUSEUM

Natural Forms

And not so natural

A leafy sheltered avenue blossom in February! Even the birdsong sounds different — exotic — in here...

light viridian green

matt inside shiny out

18

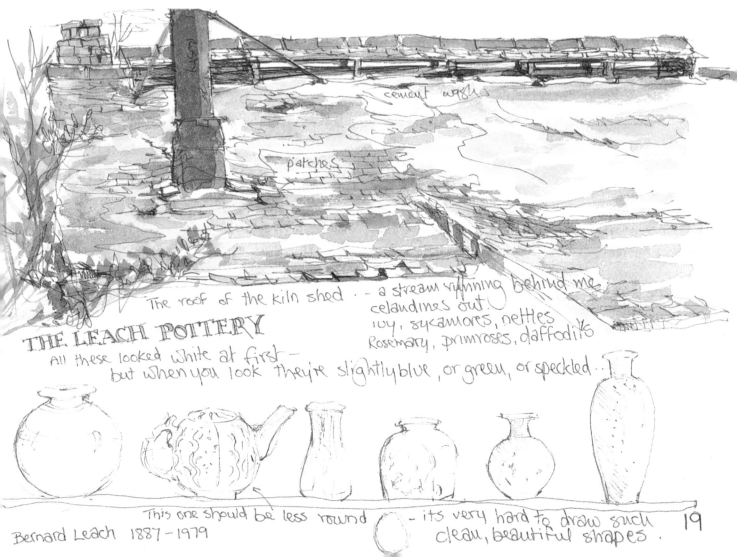

The roof of the kiln shed · · a stream running behind me.
celandines out.
ivy, sycamores, nettles
Rosemary, primroses, daffodils

cement wash

patches

THE LEACH POTTERY

All these looked white at first —
but when you look they're slightly blue, or green, or speckled ··

This one should be less round — its very hard to draw such
clean, beautiful shapes.

Bernard Leach 1887-1979

21

22

23

Godrevy

PORTH GWIDDEN - very hot & sheltered

Pink legs, white spots on Tail

24

A helicopter hovering & then disappearing
behind the Island

Redruth!

blue hills
The Towans

Just the shadows of sunbathers

blue
yellow
green
pink

25

GALLERIES

outside, looking in

31   PIER

EASIDE
SKETCHBOOK

Inside, looking out.

26

THE ST. IVES
SCHOOL OF PAINTING

27

VIEW FROM THE TATE
Seagulls over the rooftops....

... and carrot cake & coffee...

.... and pictures.

behind me is a painting by Wallis
called 'Wreck of the Alba'
painted around
1939...

blue green glass

ough the window I can
the boiler of the
ba still on Porthmeor
Beach

Barbara Hepworth 1903-1975
CURVED FORM
(Trevalgan)
sculpture in bronze
ky & sea blend with hills&
ks, the forms seem to enfold
a watcher & lift him
rds the sky."

very dark - almost green

A wonderful distorted
reflection of houses
- just like a painting

THE TATE

29

Inside the Parish Church

Barbara Hepworth's Madonna & child in the Lady Chapel

bright blue

The choir stalls - these 15th century panels may have been part of the original Rood Screen

SAINT · IA

black
gold

white
green

purple
gold
red
silver
green

she also designed the candlesticks

Saint Ia - who sailed into St. Ives on a leaf in the 5th or 6th century

30

ST. NICHOLAS CHAPEL   The island.

"which has stood upon this site from time immemorial"
I can see past Godrevy - line upon line of cliffs & headlands,
then round the Bay & all of St Ives to Porthmeor & Clodgy Point

looking back over the town

31

Anchors & nets,
buoys & pots'

Sitting on Smeaton's Pier

A large seal just swam casually in among the boats
right below me.

THE SLOOP INN
The last of the ancient inns in the
Harbour. The others are now
shops.

33

John & Debbie's stained glass in the Sloop Market

And more starfish & shells . . . & shells . . . in fore g . . .

Hot sun, strong shadows

Tulips 𝑟

buckets 𝑟 spades —
These two had to go together.

36

scantle slates

cement wash

yellow lichen

The backs of shops. tile-hung r weed-grown . . . .

Near Westcott's Quay

Near the Pier

37

38

Morning light across the sand.
low spring tide

40

41

February - sunshine, calm sea
lots of people enjoying the weather,
watching the sea...

Behind us the town is busy
getting ready for the summer
but out here its just the gulls

lots of children chasing across the
sand & disappearing into the town...

Feast Monday - the first Monday after
3rd February - the anniversary of the
consecration of the Parish Church in 1434.
Hurling is played by the schoolchildren. The silver
ball is thrown by the Mayor at 10.30 & the child who
returns it at noon receives a reward.

carrying the silver ball....

Dancing through the streets to the church

FEAST DAY   February 9th.

43

Lazy lunchtime, sunny r warm. Visitors watching boats r gulls watching visitors

44

A perfect spot on the wharf for quiet contemplation

sorting out the picnic

especially if you've brought your own chair

45

There are cats everywhere. Some of the sketches have been drawn with a black cat who lives in Virgin Street on my lap...

46

SEA FOOD SHOP

SPECIAL
FRESH LOCAL
COD + HADDOCK
FILLETS
1·90

WIND AN SEA
SURFING CENTRE

CORNISH ICE CREAM   Made in Cornwall
CORNISH WHIPPY   CORNISH WHIPPY

The YELLOW CANARY
SANDWICH BAR

★ CORNISH ★
CREAM
TEAS ☆

Cornish
Clotted Cream   strawberry jam
2·75   pot of tea
Two Scones

BUY 8 GET 2 FREE

CHICKEN TIKKA
CHEEZ
CHEESE + BACON   VEGETARIAN   TRADITIONAL

PORTHMEOR
sun, sand r surfers . . . .

48